WORLD'S WORST...

FIRE Disasters

Louise Spilsbury
Rob Alcraft

Heinemann
Schools Library and Information Service

www.heinemann.co.uk
Visit our website to find out more information about **Heinemann Library** books.

To order:
☎ Phone 44 (0) 1865 888066
▤ Send a fax to 44 (0) 1865 314091
▥ Visit the Heinemann Bookshop at www.heinemann.co.uk to browse our catalogue and order online.

First published in Great Britain by Heinemann Library,
Halley Court, Jordan Hill, Oxford OX2 8EJ
a division of Reed Educational and Professional Publishing Ltd.

Heinemann is a registered trademark of Reed Educational & Professional Publishing Ltd.

OXFORD MELBOURNE AUCKLAND JOHANNESBURG BLANTYRE GABORONE IBADAN
PORTSMOUTH (NH) USA CHICAGO

Designed by Celia Floyd
Illustrations by David Cuzik (Pennant Illustrations) and Jeff Edwards
Originated by Dot Gradations, UK
Printed by Wing King Tong, in Hong Kong

ISBN 0 431 01288 1 (hardback)   ISBN 0 431 01295 4 (paperback)
04 03 02 01 00   04 03 02 01 00
10 9 8 7 6 5 4 3 2   10 9 8 7 6 5 4 3 2 1

British Library Cataloguing in Publication Data

Alcraft, Rob, 1966–
  World's worst fire disasters
  1.Fires – Juvenile literature
  I.Title II.Spilsbury, Louise III.Fire disasters
  363.3'7

Acknowledgements

The Publishers would like to thank the following for permission to reproduce photographs: AKG: p.5; Colorific!: Penny Tweedie p.21; Corbis: p.14, Bettmann p.15, p.18, James L Amos p.7; Heinemann: Chris Honeywell p.27; Image Select: p.13; Museum of London: p.8, p.9, p.12; Rex Features: p.29; Still Pictures: Mark Edwards p.25; Tony Stone: Paul Edmondson p.4, Gary Irving p.26, S & N Geary p.20, Richard Kaylin p.6; Topham Picturepoint: Associated Press p.24.

Cover photograph reproduced with permission of Mitch Kezar: Tony Stone.

Our thanks to Dr Henry Wilson of the International Journal of Disaster Prevention and Management, Department of Industrial Technology, University of Bradford for his comments in the preparation of this book.

Every effort has been made to contact copyright holders of any material reproduced in this book. Any omissions will be rectified in subsequent printings if notice is given to the Publisher.

Any words appearing in the text in bold, **like this**, are explained in the Glossary.

Contents

Fire

People have used fire for thousands of years. Fire is our friend, but it is also our enemy. It keeps us warm, makes light for us to see by and cooks our food. But it also kills and destroys.

In some parts of the world farmers use fire to keep wild animals away from their cattle and goats. In the Amazon rainforest local Indians use controlled fires to burn back the trees. When the fire is gone farmers can use the land for growing crops. Or if they leave the land, new tender shoots grow, and when animals come to feed off these, the Indians hunt them for food.

Amazonian Indians know how to live in the rainforest without ruining it. Sadly, some ranchers, often from companies based abroad, are burning vast areas of the forest to raise cattle or crops on. Because of this, the rainforest is in danger of being lost altogether.

Controlled burning of small areas of the rainforest which is used by the Amazonian Indians, does not hurt the environment.

Dresden in ruins after fire-bomb attacks during World War II.

Deadly weapon

Fire is used to kill too, sometimes as a weapon of war. In World War II cities such as Tokyo in Japan, and Dresden in Germany were fire-bombed. The intention of the bombing was to destroy the cities. It worked. The fire that engulfed Tokyo could be seen 240 km away, and killed around 200,000 people. In Dresden the fire-bombing created a scorching 160 km per hour wind as the flames sucked air into the city. The entire city was burned, and around 400,000 people died.

Fire disasters

In this book we look at three of the worst fire disasters in history. We look at how the fires started, and how they spread. Using eyewitness accounts of survivors and the reports of experts we look at what happened, and how the fires leapt out of control. Are there lessons that we should all learn from such disasters?

5

Nowhere to Hide

Fires can happen almost anywhere. Fire destroys plants and animals in forests and grasslands all over the world. Flames swallow buildings, large and small, in villages, towns and cities every day. Fires occur under the ground in mines and underground railways, and under the sea in tunnels deep below the waves. They can even attack in the air, in planes full of highly **inflammable** fuel. Most of the time we are safe – all over the world extensive fire precautions are taken and followed. Sometimes, despite all the measures taken to prevent fires, mistakes are made and accidents happen.

Fire-fighters at airports use a special foam, which is very safe, to put out aircraft fires like this one.

Fighting fire

Early fire-fighters used horse-drawn carts, and water poured by hand-pumps or buckets to stop a blaze. Today's modern fire services have breathing apparatus, remote cameras and lifting equipment. Modern water pumps can shoot thousands of litres of water onto a fire every minute and fire-fighters may also use foam or other special substances to stop certain fires.

Forest fires

Today, forest rangers in larger forest areas have special towers from where they watch for fires. In some places rangers fly over vast forests or grasslands to check for signs of danger. If there is a fire, highly trained and organized teams use trucks to carry water to put out the flames and bulldozers to clear **fire-breaks**. They may also use helicopters and planes to drop water.

City fires

Fire-fighters today are helped by modern building design and materials. The brick, stone, concrete and metals used for building materials today are **non-combustible** compared to those used in the past. Modern safety standards ensure that public buildings have **fire-doors** and **fire-extinguishers**. They are also designed so that fire cannot spread quickly through a building.

Flash-over

Flash-over is the name for the way a fire can leap through buildings. A flash-over is the smoke and gas from a fire igniting suddenly in a wall of moving flame. It is one of the most dangerous things a fire-fighter can face. A flash-over will kill or badly burn anyone in normal clothing. Even the protective clothing worn by modern fire-fighters cannot completely protect them from the intense heat. Fire-fighters today learn to recognize the signs that can show them a fire is about to flash-over.

Special suits like this protect today's fire-fighters from the heat and dangerous fumes given off by most fires.

Devastation!
The Great Fire of London, 1666

UK •London

On Sunday 2 September 1666 a small fire at a baker's in Pudding Lane, London grew out of control. The flames ate away at the city for four days. Amazingly, only eight people died, but more than half the area within the city walls was destroyed, including 13,200 houses, 87 churches and most of London's major public buildings.

London

In 1666 London was the second largest city in Europe. Most of its 450,000 inhabitants lived in houses and worked in shops and warehouses built of wood and **thatch**, packed closely together along narrow streets and alleys. Most people had stores of wood and other fuel for lighting, heating and cooking. Everything was dry after a long, hot summer. London in September 1666 was a tightly packed **tinder-box** waiting to burn.

This model of London at the time of the Great Fire shows how tightly packed the wooden houses in the city were.

As London burned, many people escaped to the river, throwing belongings into the river or onto carts as they fled.

Small beginnings

Before going to bed that fateful night, baker Thomas Farrinor checked that the fires in his bakehouse ovens were out. But smouldering **embers** ignited fuelwood stored nearby, and sometime after 1 am the house was alight. The family and a servant escaped across the rooftops. The family's maid, fearful of the dangerous climb, stayed behind and became the first victim of the flames.

The wooden, **pitch**-covered buildings nearby ignited at the touch of the smallest spark and the warehouses at the quayside were full of **combustibles** such as timber, oil and rope. A strong east wind fanned the flames and carried burning embers and debris on to other buildings, setting them alight. The speed at which the fire spread made it almost impossible to fight. The fire chased people from their homes, swallowing everything in its path. By the time the fire was put out on Thursday afternoon, London was in ruins.

Samuel Pepys, a government official in London, was a famous diarist. This is taken from his entry for 2 September.

(We) stayed there till it was dark almost and saw the fire grow... in corners and upon steeples and between churches and houses as far as we could see up the hill of the City, in a most horrid malicious bloody flame...and a horrid noise the flames made, and the cracking of houses at their ruin.

London's Burning

Londoners were well aware of the risks of fire – a fire at an inn stable in Southwark in 1630 had destroyed 50 houses, and in 1633 a third of the houses on London Bridge and 80 nearby had been wrecked by flames. But people in the city thought they were well prepared. In all **parishes** there were stores of hooked poles for pulling down burning roofs or houses, pumps and water squirts and leather buckets for **dousing** blazes. But nothing could have prepared them for the **inferno** of 1666.

England

River Thames

Key

London – present day

London – before 1666 fire

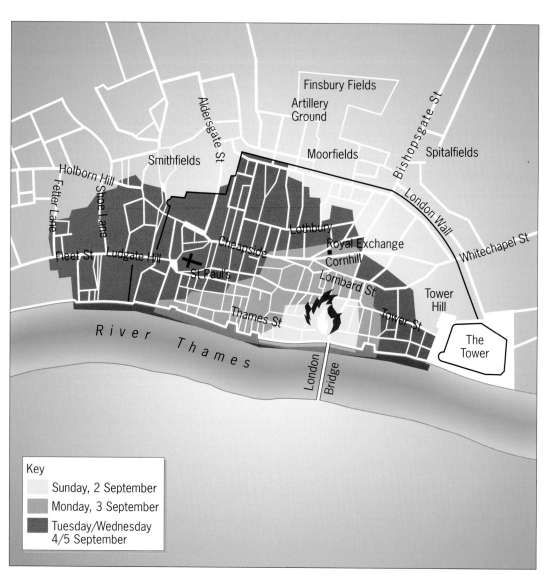

Finsbury Fields

Artillery Ground

Aldersgate St

Smithfields

Moorfields

Bishopsgate St

Spitalfields

Holborn Hill

Shoe Lane

London Wall

Fetter Lane

Lothbury

Cheapside

Royal Exchange

Whitechapel St

Fleet St

Ludgate Hill

Cornhill

St Paul's

Lombard St

Thames St

Tower St

Tower Hill

The Tower

R i v e r   T h a m e s

London Bridge

Key

Sunday, 2 September

Monday, 3 September

Tuesday/Wednesday 4/5 September

1 Sunday. At about 2am a fire in a Pudding Lane bakehouse spreads to nearby houses. The Lord Mayor, Sir Thomas Bludworth, is alerted. He declares the fire will be easy to put out and that there is no need to pull down houses to make a **fire-break**. The fire spreads to nearby streets, and warehouses on the quayside.

2 By 4am a strong wind urges the flames on – about 100 houses are burned every hour. Fire-fighters throw water from buckets, but the heat stops them getting very close. The king, Charles I, orders Bludworth to tear down houses to create fire-breaks. But many people are reluctant to allow this and fire-breaks are made too close to the front of the fire to be any use. The fire is beyond control. Londoners flee.

3 Monday. Driven by the east wind the fire moves west towards Fleet River and north beyond Cornhill and the Royal Exchange, the business centre of the city. The king puts the Duke of York in charge. His guards organize fire-breaks, and try to keep the peace and prevent **looting**.

4 Tuesday morning. **Militia** arrive from outside London to help fight the fire. Cheapside is destroyed and half the city is in flames. St Paul's Cathedral is lost to the inferno. Flames up to 100m high reach halfway up Fleet Street. Gunpowder is used to clear fire-breaks which save the Tower of London.

5 Wednesday. The fire reaches Temple and Cripplegate, but the wind drops and it goes no further. Although the fire still burns, the improved conditions make it possible to start tackling it. By the end of the day all fires in the west are extinguished.

6 Thursday. With most of the fires out, all resources are concentrated on the remaining flames. A further outbreak at Temple is put down by 2am. By the end of the day the Great Fire is over at last.

What Went Wrong?

How did a fire which began so small destroy a city?
Parliament set up a committee to investigate. Its report found
that the fire began at Farrinor's bakehouse, but concluded
that the extent of the devastation was caused by 'the hand of
God upon us, a great wind and the season so very dry.'

These Engins, (which are ⸻ the best) to quinch great Fires; are

Out of control

But the wind and the dryness of the season did not explain
why the fire was not tackled more efficiently. One reason
was that it began in the middle of the night, when people
slept. Also it was Sunday, when fewer people than usual
were up early. Action was only taken when the fire had
grown too fierce to be controlled. Many people said that
the responsibility lay with Lord Mayor Bludworth, who did
not act as quickly or firmly as he should have done, so
fire-breaks were made too late.

Although fire-fighting
equipment, like this
engine designed in
1658, was available, it
was not much use
because it was not used
soon enough and it
could not carry very
much water.

12

After the fire

Most people had lost everything. 100,000 people spent a harsh winter living in makeshift shelters and tents. Many people had no clothes other than what they wore, and had nothing to cook with. Churches raised some relief funds and the government organized financial and other assistance. But it was a hard winter for many.

After a relatively slow start – only 150 houses were built in the first year – most new building was completed within five years. And when the new City was rebuilt, it was undoubtedly a safer and healthier place to live. Houses were made of stone, brick and tile on wider streets with better **sanitation**.

God's punishment?

It was commonly accepted that the fire was God's punishment. A statue in memory of the disaster said that the fire started in Pudding Lane as a warning against 'the sin of gluttony'. A report in *The London Gazette* on 10 September said the fire was: 'the heavy hand of God upon us for our sins, showing us the terror of his judgement.' When the wind dropped so the fire could be put out, people believed God was at last showing mercy.

After the Great Fire **architect** Christopher Wren designed 52 new **parish** churches and rebuilt St Paul's Cathedral, now a famous London landmark.

A City Burns
The Chicago Fire of 1871

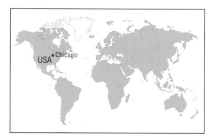

On 8 October 1871 a barn fire in Chicago, USA, raged out of control. After two days of destruction 300 people were dead, 100,000 people were homeless and offices, public buildings and factories were wrecked.

Chicago before the fire

Chicago in 1871 was a bustling and vibrant city. Nestled between the manufacturing east and the farming west of America, and linked to the west and east coasts by rail, Chicago was ideally situated to become a great economic and business centre. Goods were made, bought and sold all within the city limits.

The branches of the Chicago River divided the city into North, South and West Divisions. There was wood all over the city. Buildings were made of or trimmed with wood, streets and pavements were lined with wood. Timber was stacked in warehouses on the quayside and wooden goods were made in mills and factories. The wooden city was dry after a parched summer which had stretched on into the autumn months – there had been barely 4 cm of rain since July.

The City of Chicago before the terrible fire of 1871.

This picture, *The Rush for Life over Randolph Steet Bridge, 1871,* was painted from a sketch made during the fire by John R Chapin.

Fire in the City

Labourer Patrick O'Leary, his wife Catherine, and their five children, lived at 13 DeKoven Street in the West Division, in the cramped back rooms of a small wooden cottage. Catherine O'Leary ran a milk business from a nearby barn. Although it is not known precisely how the fire started, it seems that sometime around 9 pm on Sunday evening, 8 October 1871, a blaze began in the vicinity of the O'Leary barn. The fire quickly spread, driven on by a fierce south-westerly wind, and headed for the city centre less than 1.5 km away. People panicked and many were killed in the resulting chaos – crushed in their homes or in the city's tunnels and bridges as they struggled to **evacuate**.

> *Wabash Avenue was utterly choked with all manner of goods and people. Everybody who had been forced from the other end of town by the advancing flames had brought some article with him, and, as further progress was delayed, if not completely stopped by the river – the bridges of which were also choked, most of them, in their panic, abandoned their burdens, so that the streets and sidewalks [pavements] presented the most astonishing wreck. Valuable oil paintings, books, pet animals, musical instruments, toys, mirrors, and bedding, were trampled underfoot.*

Eyewitness and New York **Assemblyman** Alexander Frear, writing in the journal the *New York World* of 15 October 1871.

A Two-Day Inferno

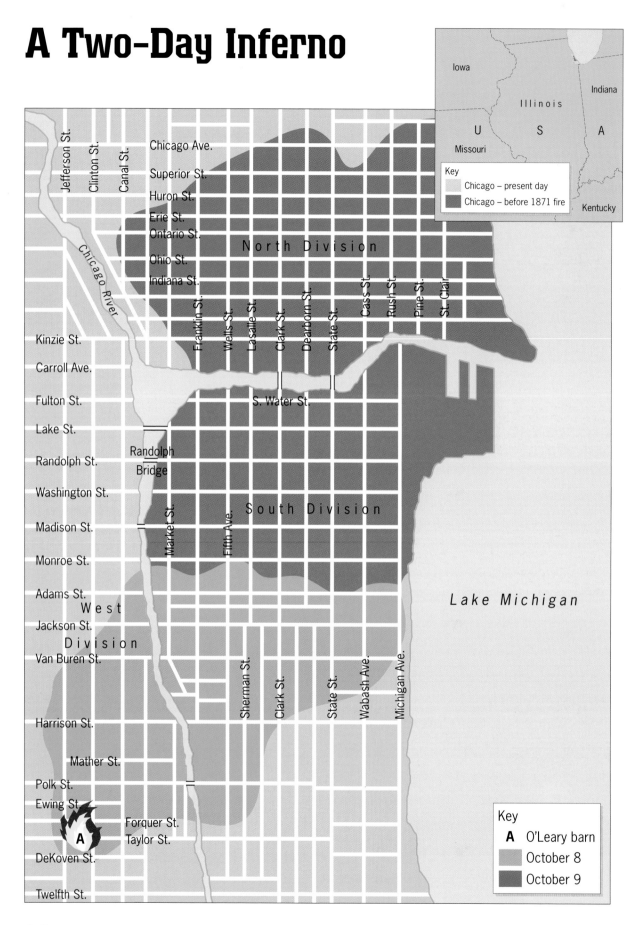

Iowa

Illinois

Indiana

U S A

Missouri

Kentucky

Key
Chicago – present day
Chicago – before 1871 fire

Jefferson St.
Clinton St.
Canal St.

Chicago Ave.
Superior St.
Huron St.
Erie St.
Ontario St.
Ohio St.
Indiana St.

North Division

Chicago River

Franklin St.
Wells St.
Lasalle St.
Clark St.
Dearborn St.
State St.
Cass St.
Rush St.
Pine St.
St. Clair

Kinzie St.
Carroll Ave.
Fulton St.
Lake St.

S. Water St.

Randolph St.
Randolph Bridge

Washington St.
Madison St.
Monroe St.

Market St.
Fifth Ave.

South Division

Adams St.
West
Jackson St.
Division
Van Buren St.

Lake Michigan

Harrison St.

Mather St.

Sherman St.
Clark St.
State St.
Wabash Ave.
Michigan Ave.

Polk St.
Ewing St.

Forquer St.
Taylor St.

A

DeKoven St.

Key
A   O'Leary barn
October 8
October 9

Twelfth St.

1 At about 9pm on Sunday 8 October a fire starts near the O'Leary family barn in the West Division. A strong south-westerly wind drives it towards the city centre. People panic and begin to flee.

2 At around midnight the wind carries blazing **embers** and smouldering debris onto new buildings to start new fires – some even jump across the south branch of the river, sparking more fires on the other side. The city is fast becoming an **inferno** – the buildings around and the wooden streets below are all in flames.

3 By 1.30am the fire reaches the courthouse tower. When officials realize that the building is going to be incinerated, they set free the prisoners inside. Thousands of people surge towards the North Division to escape, but the fire is fast catching up with them. The fire is spreading west and north now.

4 By 3am the fire is moving up Huron Street, devouring houses as it goes. At 3.30am the pumping station on that street is wrecked, ruining any chances of fighting the fire from this site.

5 By midday on Monday the fires in the North Division reach North Avenue, then Fullerton Avenue and then to the northern edge of the city.

6 By Tuesday morning rain starts to fall. The flames are quenched at last. Chicago is left smouldering and devastated.

The Aftermath of Disaster

By the time the fire was finally quenched by the rain, two days after it began, it had incinerated a vast area – 6.5km long and on average over 1km wide. Around 45km of streets had been lost along with 192km of pavements and 18,000 buildings. After the fire survivors, rich and poor alike, made equal by the losses inflicted by the fire, escaped on to any safe stretches of land they could find.

Chicago remained scorching hot for almost two days. Indeed, newspapers reported that when businessmen returned and opened their safes, the money inside, which had survived the **inferno**, burst into flames on contact with the baking hot air. Incredibly, when people did explore the city to assess the damage, they found that although the O'Leary family barn had been reduced to ashes, their cottage was still standing!

Chicago lies in ruins after the fire of 1871.

A preventable disaster?

The Chicago disaster could have been prevented if only the O'Leary barn fire had been extinguished in good time. Chicago fire-fighters were well equipped and experienced – the city had suffered and successfully put out an average of two fires a day in the previous year. However, there had been a particularly large fire the night before, on Saturday 7 October. Fire-fighters were exhausted, and perhaps because of this they were slower to respond.

In addition to this, a chance mistake helped to turn a misfortune into a tragedy. Fire-fighters alerted to the blaze at the barn were directed to the wrong neighbourhood. By the time they reached the O'Leary barn the fire was way beyond control.

The hand of God?

No single person was ever convicted of causing the Chicago disaster. Instead, it seems, a series of minor mistakes and delays was to blame. And, as in the Great Fire of London, people saw the hand of God at work. The Mayor of Chicago set aside Sunday 29 October as 'a special day of humiliation and prayer; of humiliation for those past offences against Almighty God, to which these severe afflictions were doubtless intended to lead our minds; of prayer for the relief and comfort of the suffering thousands in our midst; for the restoration of our material prosperity, especially for our lasting improvement as a people in reverence and obedience to God.'

Rebuilding the city

Luckily for the residents of Chicago, America and its developing industries had invested too much time and money in their city to let it die. Chicago still had two of the most important ingredients for future success – location and resources. Within six weeks, rebuilding was well underway. Town planners had learned their lessons from the fire – new homes were divided from factories and offices in the centre and built out of less **combustible** materials than the old ones.

Black Tuesday

Bushfires around Hobart, Tasmania, February 1967

In just under five hours on Tuesday 7 February 1967, ferocious **bushfires** around Hobart, Tasmania, burned across an area of 264,270 hectares. Over 1400 homes were destroyed and 62 people were killed. It was one of the worst fires ever recorded in the history of the country.

An area at risk

Hobart is the capital city of Tasmania, an **island state** of Australia. The city nestles between Mount Wellington to the west and the Derwent River. The river provides a natural harbour and its shoreline is fringed with picturesque bays and headlands. Hobart is surrounded by large expanses of forest and grassland.

An aerial view of Hobart and the surrounding area.

Bush fires are a frequent occurence throughout Australia, particularly after droughts. They can leave destruction in their wake.

Devastating fires

On Tuesday morning there were about 110 small fires burning, some started accidentally and others lit on purpose. At around 11am a strong wind suddenly fanned these into violent blazes which swept into the Hobart area, across the slopes of Mount Wellington and right down to the edges of the city.

Whole hillsides seemed to explode when dense clutches of burning **embers**, carried by the wind, showered down. In some places huge fireballs of burning gas rolled ahead of the main fires, crossing roads and **fire-breaks**. Pockets of unburned gas were blown across the sky. When these were ignited by smouldering embers they exploded in mid-air with a deafening roar.

The fire danger index

The hottest months in the Australian summer are January and February. The summer of 1967 had brought severe **drought** and the Hobart area was parched – ready to be ignited by the slightest spark.

Meteorologists rate the likelihood of fire in a fire danger index. Factors which contribute to risk are drought, high wind speed, high fuel levels (the amount of **combustible** plant-life or goods in a region) and low **humidity**. In February 1967 the Hobart region had all these things, giving it a fire danger index rating of 100 – the severest recorded there in 70 years!

The Flames Take Hold

The night of 6–7 February had been mild and the early morning air was relatively damp, leaving plant-life in the forested areas quite moist. It took until nearly midday for these trees and grasses to dry out. When they did, what had been small, apparently insignificant fires were stoked into life by changing winds and disaster unfolded.

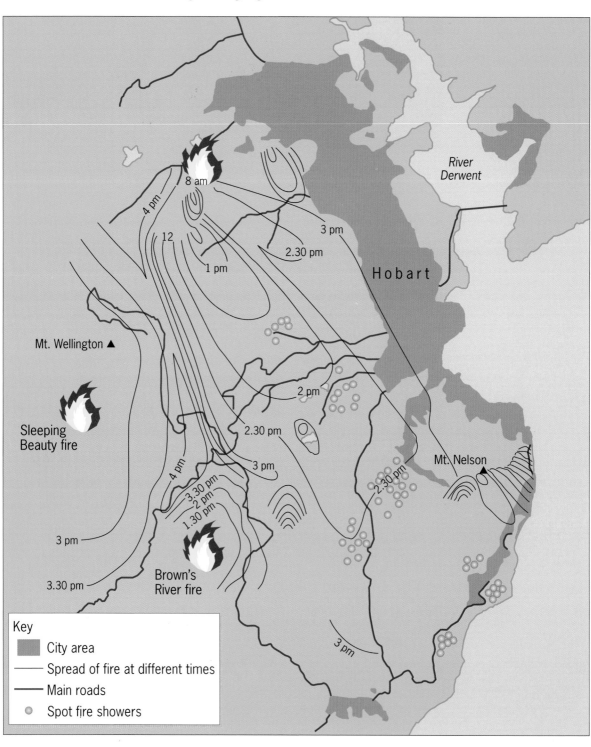

River Derwent

8 am

4 pm

12

1 pm

3 pm

2.30 pm

Hobart

Mt. Wellington ▲

2 pm

Sleeping Beauty fire

2.30 pm

3 pm

Mt. Nelson ▲

4 pm

2.30 pm

3.30 pm
2 pm
1.30 pm

3 pm

3 pm

Brown's River fire

3.30 pm

3 pm

Key

City area

Spread of fire at different times

Main roads

Spot fire showers

1   Around 11am gale-force winds blow up. Grasses and trees have dried out completely now, and the Hobart area is extremely hot and dry. Small fires which have been smouldering in the area suddenly burst into violent activity.

2   At 12am fires in forest country advance swiftly, speeded by the wind. Wind-blown **embers** from these forest blazes create **spot fires** ahead of the main fire. Often trees are not completely stripped of leaves because the wind is so strong it blows out fires in the treetops.

3   After 1pm there is a tremendous increase in the amount of land covered by flames. Some fires run into the back of each other to become an ever-advancing wall of flames. The main fires are reaching a peak of destruction. Within two hours, between 1 and 3pm, 135,000 acres of grassland and forest country are burnt.

4   Between 2 and 4pm the high winds shift direction dramatically from the south-west to the north-east. This proves to be disastrous. Many fires which were previously separate, are now blown together. Lives are lost at this time because people are trapped where fires suddenly meet, finding their escape routes barred by more flames. There is nothing standing in the way of the fires blazing in much of the open grassland and areas of small forests, so the fires in these regions burn freely.

5   Around 3pm severe fire **whirlwinds** develop on the slopes of Mount Wellington, and the Hobart and Sleeping Beauty fires start to draw together. The Hobart fire reaches the western edge of the city.

6   By 4pm some fires die out when they reach the sea and run out of fuel. Others are finally extinguished by the efforts of fire-fighters and volunteers.

After the Fire

Over 1300 homes were wrecked by the fire as well as 128 other major buildings such as factories, churches and schools. Farmers lost lands and livestock, and communications systems, such as road, rail, and telephone, were wrecked.

After the fire, investigations into its causes began. The Police Department, Hobart City Council, the Forestry Commission, Fire Brigades and other government authorities were all involved. Witnesses were interviewed and photographs were taken from aeroplanes to track the progress of the fire. Gradually the pieces of the puzzle that led to the disaster were put together.

A distraught family surveys the ruins of their home.

Children were safe

Incredibly, no children or young people were killed by the Hobart fires. Most were at school at the peak time of the fires and schoolteachers acted quickly to ensure their safety. An entry from the journal of the head teacher of Lauderdale school, near the Rokeby area, reads: *'This afternoon a fierce fire was seen approaching the school from the Rokeby area. A decision was made to **evacuate** the school to the beach as there was doubt in my mind as to whether the school would be safe.'*

24

Who started the fires?

The investigations found that of the 110 fires known to have been burning that morning, only 22 started accidentally. Eight started as **spot fires** caused by big fires in the north-west and west of Tasmania. The other 14 started for a number of different reasons, such as sparks escaping from fires at rubbish tips or **incinerators**. The rest of the fires had been deliberately lit.

Why were the fires lit?

Most of the fires were lit for **land management**. Some were started to clear ground in order to encourage new growth for animals to feed on. Some were lit to get rid of **inflammable** debris from forest floors. In some cases it was impossible to see why fires were started, leading investigators to believe that at least of few must have been lit as acts of **arson**.

Bushfires

Some **bushfires** are caused by natural events, such as lightning. However, most are caused by human carelessness, such as dropping a lit match. Australians are constantly reminded to take care with fires. In rural areas volunteers are trained to be fire-fighters in case of emergencies, and **fire-breaks** are cleared. There are also fire-spotting towers dotted across the landscape. Summer is a dangerous time – not only is the area dry and hot, but also a lot of tourists may not be so aware of fire hazards.

Fire-fighters clear a fire-break in a forested area.

Recognizing Dangers

Most fires are caused by carelessness. The fires we have seen in this book show that even minor mistakes can be disastrous.

House hazards

There are over 50,000 house fires in the UK every year. Nearly half of them are caused by cooking, and around 5000 by cigarettes or cigarette lighters.

House fires

The danger of a house fire is that it can grow very quickly, and once it takes hold it is often unstoppable. Poisonous gases and smoke collect inside a building, and the fire creates intense heat. A typical house fire can burn at 3300°C (5972°F). Heat like this can ignite walls and furniture many metres away from the original fire. A house can become an **inferno** in minutes.

'During the early stages of a fire the signs can be quite small,' says Professor David Purser of the UK's Building Research Establishment. 'Even when they become more obvious people may just carry on what they were doing, and put themselves in extreme danger. One of the problems is that people don't often recognize how fast fires can grow.'

A small fire can grow rapidly to become an uncontrollable blaze which kills hundreds of people, or engulfs a building in minutes.

Modern fire-fighters use long, extending ladders and power hoses to put out a house fire.

A standard house smoke alarm. Smoke alarms are easy to fit and can save lives.

Limiting the risks

What makes fire so dangerous is the way people ignore the risks. People often don't take fire seriously enough until it is too late. For example, many people don't bother to fit a smoke alarm, even though these are cheap and save lives. Fire is not predictable, but plans can be made to fight it. Equipment such as **fire-extinguishers** or water hoses can be kept on hand. Fire risks, such as piles of rubbish, can be cleared away. People can be trained, and buildings designed so that people can get out quickly if there is a fire.

Invisible danger

In most house fires people are not killed by the flames, but by smoke and gas. Carbon monoxide (CO) is particularly deadly. This colourless, odourless and invisible gas is responsible for most fire deaths. It can kill in minutes, and most victims fall unconscious without ever knowing what has happened.

Simple smoke alarms are the best way to avoid being overcome by the smoke and gas produced by fire. Most alarms cannot detect CO (though some are specially designed to do this), but they do warn of the smoke that a fire produces with gases like CO. Fire safety experts say all families should make sure they having working smoke alarms in their houses.

The World's Worst Fire Disasters

Sadly, there have been many thousands of fire disasters around the world. Those listed here are a selection of some of the worst, chosen because of the destruction they caused or the number of lives that were lost.

Rome, 18 July AD 64 Ten of Rome's fourteen regions were destroyed or badly damaged by fire.

Great Fire of London, Britain, 2-5 September 1666 Fire destroyed 13,200 houses and 87 parish churches. 100,000 people were made homeless. It is thought only eight people were killed.

La Compania Church, Santiago, Chile, 8 December 1863 A lamp caught fire during a service and the church burned. Over 2500 people were trapped inside and died.

The Great Chicago Fire, USA, 8-10 October 1871 A fire spreads quickly through the city killing about 300 people, and destroying 100,000 homes.

Hamburg, Germany, 25-28 July 1943 Bombing during World War II created a firestorm that killed 45,000 people and destroyed the city.

Dresden, Germany, 13-17 February 1945 Bombing raids during World War II created a firestorm that killed between 150,000 and 400,000 people. The city was destroyed.

Tokyo, Japan, 9-10 March 1945 Bombing raids during World War II created a firestorm that killed between 80,000 and 200,000 people. The city was destroyed.

Tasmanian bushfires, Australia, 7 February 1967 The 'Black Tuesday' **bushfires** destroyed over 1400 homes and killed 62 people.

Grand Hotel, Las Vegas, USA, 21 November 1980 Fire in a hotel and casino killed 100 people and injured 600 others.

Salang Pass Tunnel, Afghanistan, 2 November 1982 Fire broke out after a crash in a mountain tunnel. Between 1000 and 2700 people were trapped inside and suffocated to death.

Ash Wednesday fires, Australia, 16 February 1983 Bushfires destroyed hundreds of homes and killed 83 people.

Bradford City Football Stadium, Britain, 11 May 1985 56 people died in a fire in the stadium and 70 were injured.

Kuwait, February – November 1991 Over 700 oil wells were burned by retreating Iraqi troops during the Gulf War.

Mandi Dabwali, India, 23 December 1995 Fire in a school tent killed 500 people.

Indonesia, 1997 Bushfires burnt up to a million hectares of forest across Indonesia. Fogs of smoke (smog) affected up to 70 million people in countries across the region.

Seen from space!

Fires in Amazonia are raging constantly as rainforest is burned and cleared. The smoke from these fires can even be seen from space!

King's Cross, London, Britain, 18 November 1987. 32 people died here in a fire at an underground train station.

Glossary

architect designer of buildings who also supervises their construction

arson when a fire is lit on purpose with the intention of causing damage to people or property

Assemblyman old-fashioned word for person who is part of a law-making council

bushfire fire in forest or shrub area, usually widespread

combustible material that burns easily

dousing pouring large amounts of water onto a fire to put it out

drought long period without rain when land becomes very dry

ember smouldering piece of wood or coal from a fire

evacuate move people from a dangerous place until the danger is over

fire-break open space of land, cleared of trees and other plantlife. The fire cannot cross the cleared area as there is no fuel to burn.

fire-door door made out of fire-resistant materials to stop a fire spreading in a building

fire-extinguisher container with a jet to spray liquid foam, chemicals or water to put out a fire

humidity amount of moisture in the air

inferno an uncrontrollable and intense fire

incinerator furnace or other container used for burning rubbish

inflammable something that catches fire easily

island state island which is not a separate country but is part of a country on the mainland

land management caring for the land; taking action to manage the land in a way which benefits people and the countryside

looting steal goods from buildings which have been abandoned because of disaster or war

meteorologist person who studies and forecasts weather conditions

militia a military force, usually formed from people not already in the armed forces

non-combustible material that does not burn easily

parish area which has its own church. This was a useful way of dividing an area into districts for the purposes of local government.

Parliament part of a country's system of government which makes it laws

pitch sticky, black tar-like substance

sanitation sewers and drains which take away the city's waste and so keep it clean

spot fire fire started away from a main fire by burning embers blown in the wind

thatch roof-covering made of straw, reeds or a similar material

tinder very dry wood used to light fires

tinder-box name for a container used to store materials, such as dry wood, used for starting fires

whirlwinds mass of air or fire which whirls quickly round and round

Index